W9-CYH-933

STEM IN ICE HOCKEY

CONNECTING STEM AND SPORTS

CONNECTING
STEM
AND SPORTS

STEM IN ICE HOCKEY

ANDREW LUKE

MASON CREST
PHILADELPHIA · MIAMI

Mason Crest
450 Parkway Drive, Suite D
Broomall, Pennsylvania 19008
(866) MCP-BOOK (toll free)

Copyright © 2020 by Mason Crest, an imprint of National Highlights, Inc. All rights reserved. No part of this publication may be reproduced or transmitted in any form or by any means, electronic or mechanical, including photocopying, recording, taping, or any information storage and retrieval system, without permission from the publisher.

First printing
9 8 7 6 5 4 3 2 1

ISBN (hardback) 978-1-4222-4336-7
ISBN (series) 978-1-4222-4329-9
ISBN (ebook) 978-1-4222-7480-4

Cataloging-in-Publication Data on file with the Library of Congress

Developed and Produced by National Highlights Inc.
Editor: Andrew Luke
Interior and cover design: Annalisa Gumbrecht, Studio Gumbrecht
Production: Michelle Luke

QR CODES AND LINKS TO THIRD-PARTY CONTENT

You may gain access to certain third-party content ("Third-Party Sites") by scanning and using the QR Codes that appear in this publication (the "QR Codes"). We do not operate or control in any respect any information, products, or services on such Third-Party Sites linked to by us via the QR Codes included in this publication, and we assume no responsibility for any materials you may access using the QR Codes. Your use of the QR Codes may be subject to terms, limitations, or restrictions set forth in the applicable terms of use or otherwise established by the owners of the Third-Party Sites. Our linking to such Third-Party Sites via the QR Codes does not imply an endorsement or sponsorship of such Third-Party Sites or the information, products, or services offered on or through the Third-Party Sites, nor does it imply an endorsement or sponsorship of this publication by the owners of such Third-Party Sites.

TABLE OF CONTENTS

KEY ICONS TO LOOK FOR:

 Words To Understand: These words with their easy-to-understand definitions will increase the reader's understanding of the text while building vocabulary skills.

 Sidebars: This boxed material within the main text allows readers to build knowledge, gain insights, explore possibilities, and broaden their perspectives by weaving together additional information to provide realistic and holistic perspectives.

 Educational Videos: Readers can view videos by scanning our QR codes, providing them with additional educational content to supplement the text. Examples include news coverage, moments in history, speeches, iconic sports moments, and much more!

 Text-Dependent Questions: These questions send the reader back to the text for more careful attention to the evidence presented there.

 Research Projects: Readers are pointed toward areas of further inquiry connected to each chapter. Suggestions are provided for projects that encourage deeper research and analysis.

 Series Glossary Of Key Terms: This back-of-the-book glossary contains terminology used throughout this series. Words found here increase the reader's ability to read and comprehend higher-level books and articles in this field.

INTRODUCTION

Ice hockey is often referred to as "the fastest game in the world." Although that point can be debated, the sport is undoubtedly fast. Players regularly skate at speeds of more than 25 mph, or 40 kph as they would measure it in the countries where ice hockey is most popular. Pucks are often propelled at speeds easily surpassing 100 mph (160 kph). What makes all of this possible? The answer is STEM.

Science, technology, engineering, and math are usually encountered in the classroom, an arena in which they are very familiar. To find that they are all just as present at an ice rink might be unexpected, but the speed and movements generated it would not be possible without STEM.

Physics is the science that plays the largest part, and in this book we will see how the three laws of motion articulated by Sir Isaac Newton in the seventeenth century affect a twenty-first-century slap shot. For that slap shot to go as fast as it does requires some high-end technology in the stick used to take it. The indoor surfaces on which hockey games are played are an engineering marvel. As for math, well, how would you know which players to drop or pick up on your fantasy hockey team without being able to calculate even-strength Corsi for percentage? Math is a must for hockey stat–heads.

STEM concepts and examples are prevalent throughout the sport of hockey. The chapters ahead will explain how players can skate so fast, shoot so hard, pass with precision, and make those incredible saves. Let's drop the puck.

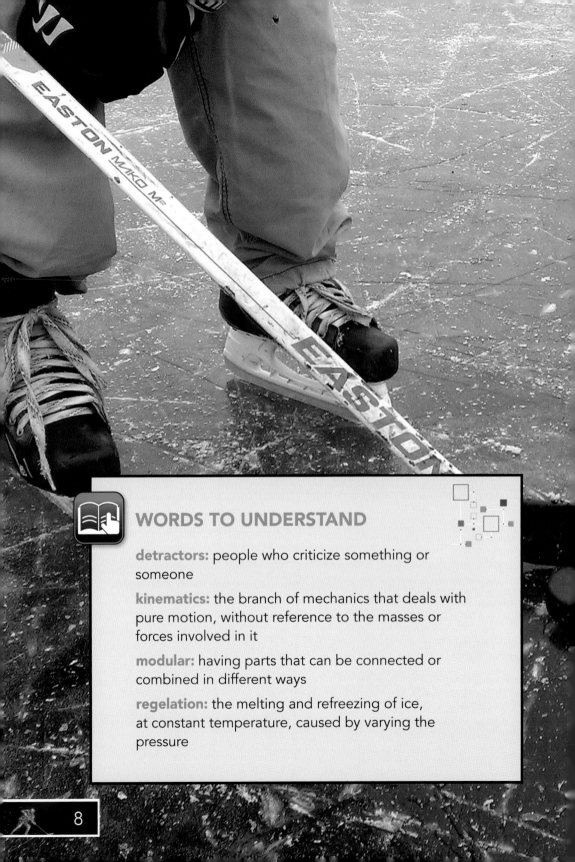

WORDS TO UNDERSTAND

detractors: people who criticize something or someone

kinematics: the branch of mechanics that deals with pure motion, without reference to the masses or forces involved in it

modular: having parts that can be connected or combined in different ways

regelation: the melting and refreezing of ice, at constant temperature, caused by varying the pressure

CHAPTER 1

SKATING

The game of hockey comes in a few different formats. There is field hockey, which is played using a hard, solid, plastic ball outdoors on large fields that are a little smaller than a soccer field. Then there is ball hockey, which is played on a surface made of hard **modular** plastic in regular-sized hockey rinks. Players use hard plastic balls, some of which are filled with a liquid that won't freeze in cold weather. Ball hockey is one of several variations of street hockey. The biggest difference between any of these other formats and ice hockey is that they are played while standing or running with your feet on solid ground rather than balancing on two thin steel blades.

Ice is the element that defines the sport, and skating is the skill that puts it a level above other formats and other sports. Certainly all sports require varying amounts of running, balance, agility, and hand-eye coordination, but not while balancing on a slippery surface. Skating adds that extra level of difficulty that other sports do not have. So how exactly can a 200 lb. (90 kg) man balance on a pair of skates? He uses science.

How does ice skating work? As this video explains, the answer is not as easy as it might appear.

Why Can We Skate on Ice?

There are a number of theories about how ice skating works. One theory, suggested by Englishman Michael Faraday in 1850, says it is due to pressure. Pressure, the force applied by the weight of the skater to the blades of the skate, reduces the melting point of the ice. As the ice melts slightly under the pressure, it leaves a thin film of water that the blades can glide on. It then refreezes when the pressure is removed. This process is known as **regelation**.

Modern scientists have disputed this pressure theory, however, asserting that even the heaviest human skater would not be able to create enough pressure to bring the ice to its melting point at temperatures colder than 26°F (–3.5°C). Another popular theory says that the answer is friction. The friction theory holds that it is the friction caused by the blade moving against the ice that generates enough heat to produce the

Bruising Winnipeg Jets defenseman Dustin Byfuglien weighs 260 lb., but even he is not heavy enough to create the pressure under his skate blades needed to melt ice.

slight melting needed for the thin water layer to glide on. This theory also has its **detractors**, who point to the simple observation that ice is slippery even when standing still on it.

Hot Metal

In theory, there should be a point on the thermometer when skating should be possible on any solid surface. As University of California–Berkeley theoretical chemistry professor David Limmer told *Vox* in 2018, all solids will form a thin liquid layer when they are close to their melting temperature. Take a substance like gallium, for example. Gallium is a metal with a very low melting point—just under 86°F (30°C). This means that, in theory, you could play hockey on a shiny, mirrorlike surface of gallium in a balmy 80°F (26.7°C) rink!

A 2015 theory by German scientist Bo Persson expanded on the friction theory, suggesting that depending on the speed at which the skater is moving, the ice will either melt or refreeze. The surface becomes one consisting of a substance that is switching between water and ice very rapidly. This still does not address the issue of why ice is slippery in the absence of friction, however.

Perhaps it is because ice is just naturally slippery or, in other words, has very low friction. The science behind this theory (put forth by a team of Dutch researchers in 2018) argues that two types of water molecules exist on the

Ice is naturally slippery because rapidly moving water molecules keep its surface layer in a liquid state.

surface of ice. They studied the surface layer using a new technique known as sum frequency generation spectroscopy. Using lasers to illuminate only the thin surface layer of the ice, researchers were able to observe the water molecules. One type of molecule is bonded to the underlying ice by three hydrogen atoms, whereas the others have only two hydrogen bonds, which allows them to move over the ice surface rapidly and constantly. This makes the surface of ice more like a liquid than a solid. As the ice becomes warmer, more and more of the three-H-bonded molecules convert to two-bonded molecules, increasing the surface mobility of the ice. The slipperiness of ice results from the level of mobility of the surface water molecules. The higher the mobility, the lower the friction.

The opposite is true as the ice gets colder—friction increases as surface mobility goes down. The slipperiness of ice starts to diminish around –22°F (–30°C). At –392°F (–200°C), ice is not very slippery: it has relatively high friction. For hockey rinks, the ideal temperature is about 16°F (–9°C). If the ice is warmer than about 19°F (–7°C), it becomes too soft, and skates dig in rather than glide.

Skating

Even though scientists are not exactly sure why we can skate on ice, we all know that it works really well. Hockey players can propel themselves at speeds up to 25 mph (40 kph). They can stop in an instant and change direction in the blink of an eye.

The mechanics behind skating primarily involve controlling the level of friction between the ice surface and the skate blades. These mechanics, called **kinematics**, explain how players are able to move across the ice. To propel themselves, skaters maximize friction by digging the blades of their push-off skate into the ice. Then they can push off by strongly exerting force with their hips and legs that is perpendicular to the skate blade, creating momentum in the direction they want to go and positioning the lead skate to point in the direction of motion. This way the blade of the lead skate is creating minimal friction. As the skater moves forward, he or she switches legs and pushes off with what was the lead skate, continuing to mirror the process with every stride. Stopping is the opposite.

Maximizing friction by turning their skate blades perpendicular to the direction of motion allows players to stop suddenly.

Instead of pointing the skate blade in the direction they are traveling, skaters turn the skates to a sudden 90-degree angle, creating maximum friction and enabling them to stop abruptly.

Velocity, or speed, is one of the key components of kinematics. Velocity, the time rate of change of position of the skater, is calculated by dividing the distance traveled in a given direction by the time it takes to travel that distance, or $v=d/t$. Acceleration is another key component. Acceleration is the measure of how much a player's speed or direction changes over a given period of time. During acceleration, velocity is constantly changing, like with a player on a breakaway trying to pull away from an opponent. Average acceleration is calculated by dividing velocity by time, or $a=v/t$. The more force a player exerts with his or her legs, the faster he or she will accelerate to maximum velocity.

Newton's First Law of Motion states that an object in motion tends to stay in motion unless acted on by an external force. Without friction, velocity would be constant after the first push-off and the skater would glide until he or she crashes into the boards. Though that is an effective way to stop, increasing friction is a much safer way to decrease velocity and stop as needed.

Have We Mentioned Friction?

Friction is again the answer when the question arises as to why hockey players are careful to make sure their skates are always sharp. A sharp skate blade has less surface area than one that is dull. This means less contact with the ice surface, and therefore less friction, allowing the skates to glide more easily going forward or backward.

What happens when the skater wants to change direction quickly or suddenly? Sharp blades also help in the opposite way as well. Sharper blades cut deeper into the ice when planted, which provides the resistance that allows skaters to stop the momentum in one direction and apply the force necessary to move in a different direction.

Hockey players can change direction suddenly by digging their blades into the ice and applying force to push off in the direction they want to go.

More Than Just Force

Of course, there is more to skating than applying force with the hips and legs to move in a given direction.

Hockey players also need to maintain balance while accelerating over the ice surface. To do this, they typically lean forward in the direction of movement. This prevents them from tipping backward when the force generated by the forward movement pushes against them. Remembering Newton's Third Law of Motion: for every action there is an equal and opposite reaction. Therefore, players need to counteract the forces working against them, such as torque (the rotational force caused by arm swing) and gravity. Leaning forward moves the center of mass forward. Center of mass is the mean position of mass in an object. Keeping it forward allows for more forward momentum.

Once a player has mastered the essential fundamentals of skating, the next hurdle is learning how to shoot. After all, you cannot win a hockey game if you do not score any goals.

Text-Dependent Questions:

1. What activity is ball hockey a variation of?

2. What happens to an ice surface when the mobility of its molecules increases?

3. According to Newton's First Law, what would happen to a skater if there were no friction?

Research Project:

Hockey is just one of many sports that uses ice skates. However, the skates used in sports such as speed skating and figure skating are quite different. Do some research to create a chart that compares and contrasts the differences in the skates. Be sure to include the scientific reasons behind these differences.

WORDS TO UNDERSTAND

composite: made up of disparate or separate parts or elements

convex: having a surface that is curved or rounded outward

intuitive: easy to understand or operate without explicit instruction

CHAPTER 2

SHOOTING

As with skating, there are some players who are better at shooting the puck than others. These players might not be the fastest or the strongest, but they just have the uncanny ability to release the puck with accuracy and power and to do it so quickly that their opponents are unprepared for it. National Hockey League (NHL) players like Joe Sakic, Alex Ovechkin, Al MacInnis, and Mike Gartner are some of the best shooters in the history of the league. They specialized in different types of shots as well. Let's examine the science and technology behind these deadly offensive weapons.

Slap Shot

The slap shot is the big shiny gem of all hockey shots. It has power, ferocity, and big impact potential that help give it great appeal for players and fans. The slap shot, the hardest of all hockey shots, is executed by striking the puck with a stick that starts from a position with the blade above the shooter's head and the shaft perpendicular to the ice.

The slap shot is the hardest shot in hockey.

Before delving into what is happening with the slap shot, it is important to understand the role of the hockey stick. It is not simply a tool but rather a high-tech marvel that is much different than the pieces of lumber used in the first several decades of organized ice hockey. Traditional wooden sticks were phased out at the professional level and replaced by aluminum models in the 1980s. Today's sticks do not use wood or aluminum at all. They are made of a **composite** of materials including carbon fiber, graphite, and fiberglass. These sticks are both lightweight and easier to duplicate precisely, which was not the case with wood.

STEM Careers

Have you ever watched an NHL game and seen your favorite player streaking in on goal only to have the stick snap in his hands when he tries to shoot and thought, "I could make a better stick than that!"? If so, you should consider a career in industrial design. More than seventy schools offer four-year degree programs in industrial design. Industrial designers work on everything from better helmets to stronger sticks and pads. Basic art skills are a must for this career. Justin Lau is an industrial designer at Warrior Hockey in Montreal. He started out building pants and gloves and moved on to making complete product lines used by players around the world, including twelve NHL team captains.

Hockey sticks have two main parts: the shaft, which is where the player holds the stick, and the blade, which is what contacts the puck. Most players choose to use blades that are curved up to three-quarters of an inch (two centimeters). The curve allows for a greater ability to put spin on the puck (more on this later). Sticks can also be designed with varying flexibility, which is measured on a scale from 110 to 40. A stick with a stiff shaft is a 110, whereas one with a lot of flex is a 40. Most NHL players use sticks that are rated 75 or higher. That number represents how much weight has to be applied to the center of a stick's shaft to deflect, or bend, a hockey stick 1 in. (2.5 cm). Bigger and stronger players tend to use stiffer sticks. Youth players typically use sticks in the 40 to 50 range.

Here is how the flexibility of the stick comes into play. When a player shoots the puck using a slap shot, the stick actually makes contact with the ice a few inches before it strikes the puck. The resistance from moving along the ice causes the

On a slap shot, the shooter makes contact with the ice at least six inches (15 cm) behind the puck. The resistance of the ice causes the stick to flex as it stores potential energy that is released in the follow-through.

stick to flex as potential energy is stored in it. This stored energy is gradually transferred to the puck upon contact. It is **intuitive** to think that the friction and drag caused by making contact with the ice before the puck would slow down the shot. The opposite, however, is true. The release of the stored potential energy in the stick is added to that of the force of swinging the stick itself, meaning the puck goes even faster than if the stick had hit it cleanly.

Players need to understand how long it takes for the transfer of energy from stick to puck to occur. Players follow through on their slap shots to allow all the potential energy to whip out of the stick. A well-taken slap shot can exceed 100 mph (160 kph).

Wrist Shot

The wrist shot is the slap shot's quieter, sneakier, and extremely effective partner. About one-quarter to one-third of all shots in professional hockey are wrist shots, and they account for more than 50 percent of goals. The shot gets its name from the action used to generate it. With the puck on the blade of the stick, the shooter applies downward pressure to the stick and flicks his or her bottom wrist forward while transferring energy to the puck.

In 2009, a couple of professors at McGill University in Montreal set out to explain the mechanics of the "wrister." Their findings centered on a concept called angular momentum, which is the change in direction of an object around a fixed point, or a measurement of an object's ability to keep spinning. The equation is

Angular momentum (L) = Moment of inertia (I) x Angular velocity (w) or $L = Iw$

One of the main differences between a wrist shot and a slap shot is how the puck comes off of the blade. This has to do with the principle of projectile motion. Projectile motion is the change in position of an object propelled into the air that is acted on only by gravity. A puck launched into the air by a hockey stick is a projectile. With the slapper, the puck is launched on impact straight ahead with upward and forward motion. With the wrister, there is no impact, but rather the puck rolls along the curve of the stick blade, meaning that when it is launched, it is spinning around its center as well as moving up and forward. This spin gives the projectile in motion angular momentum. The more angular momentum a puck has, the more it will continue to spin.

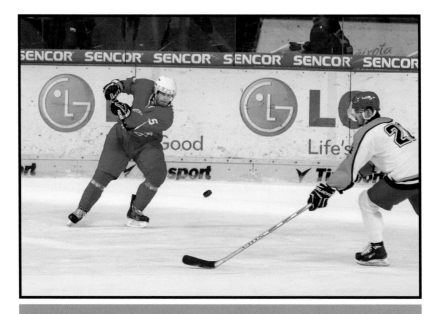

The more angular momentum a puck has when it is shot, the more it will continue to spin.

The law of conservation of angular momentum states that angular momentum is conserved when there is zero net torque applied to a system where the system is the object that is rotating. Net torque multiplied by a change in time will produce a change in angular momentum, or $\Delta L = t\Delta t$. Torque is the twisting force that causes rotation. Without torque, angular momentum will remain unchanged, or be conserved. Therefore, after the puck leaves the stick blade, if no additional torque is applied, the puck will continue to rotate through the air. The spinning motion allows the puck to more easily cut through air molecules without being displaced, which makes it more stable and therefore more likely to maintain its trajectory. The extra contact time the shooter has with the puck on the blade with the wrist shot (compared to the slap shot) gives the shooter that much more time and control to determine the trajectory more accurately. It is the spin that gives the stability to the trajectory of the puck. This is why the wrist shot is easier to control than the slap shot. It favors accuracy over power.

NHL superstar and 2017 Rookie of the Year Auston Matthews demonstrates his deadly wrist shot.

Quick Release

Perhaps even more important than accuracy on a wrist shot is the speed with which the shooter is able to take the shot. Being able to release a shot quickly gives the shooter the advantage over the goaltender because it minimizes the time the goaltender has to prepare to save the shot. Getting the shot off quickly, or having a quick release, is a skill in its own right. A 2017 poll of NHL players determined that Vladimir Tarasenko of St. Louis is thought to have the quickest release of current NHL players. Other players mentioned include 2019 NHL scoring champion Nikita Kucherov of Tampa Bay and Patrik Laine of Winnipeg. These players all possess the ability to go from a puck-carrying or puck-receiving position to a shooting position very quickly.

Snap Shot

Unlike the slap shot, which requires a big windup, the wrist shot can be fired using a quick release. Another shot that is also released quickly is the snap shot. This is a little like a slap shot with no windup. The shooter brings the blade back only

The snap shot is especially effective close to the goal.

about a foot (30 cm) before snapping the puck by transferring his or her weight to the skate on the opposite side of the blade while quickly pulling the top hand back and pushing the bottom hand forward. This shot lacks the accuracy of the wrist shot because the puck does not spin. It also lacks the power of the slap shot because there is minimal windup or stick flex. Therefore, the snap shot is most effective closest to the net. Its advantage is deception. Unlike both the slapper and even the wrister, it is difficult for goalies to anticipate. It is not a hard shot, but close to the net when the goalie is not expecting it, the snap shot can be very effective.

Backhand

Another shot players will use when in close quarters with the goaltender is the backhand. This refers to shots taken using the backside of the stick, where the blade is **convex**. The math shows how effective this shot can be in tight. As figure 1 illustrates, the slap shot is most effective outside of 30 ft. (9 m), because at that distance the puck needs to be traveling quickly or the goaltender will have too much time to get in position to stop it. Inside 30 ft., the wrist shot dominates due to its accuracy, whereas the snap shot becomes a factor as well. Notice that inside 20 ft, (6 m), the backhand is the second-most effective shot, accounting for 19 percent of all goals (the wrist shot is at 63 percent) at this distance.

Figure 1

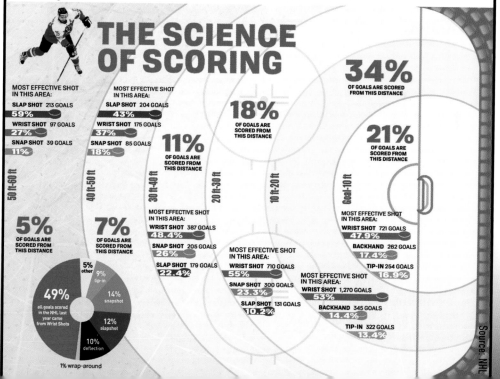

THE SCIENCE OF SCORING

MOST EFFECTIVE SHOT IN THIS AREA:
SLAP SHOT 213 GOALS — 59%
WRIST SHOT 97 GOALS — 27%
SNAP SHOT 39 GOALS — 11%

MOST EFFECTIVE SHOT IN THIS AREA:
SLAP SHOT 204 GOALS — 43%
WRIST SHOT 175 GOALS — 37%
SNAP SHOT 85 GOALS — 18%

18% OF GOALS ARE SCORED FROM THIS DISTANCE

11% OF GOALS ARE SCORED FROM THIS DISTANCE

34% OF GOALS ARE SCORED FROM THIS DISTANCE

21% OF GOALS ARE SCORED FROM THIS DISTANCE

50 ft–60 ft

40 ft–50 ft

30 ft–40 ft

20 ft–30 ft

10 ft–20 ft

Goal–10 ft

5% OF GOALS ARE SCORED FROM THIS DISTANCE

7% OF GOALS ARE SCORED FROM THIS DISTANCE

MOST EFFECTIVE SHOT IN THIS AREA:
WRIST SHOT 387 GOALS — 48.4%
SNAP SHOT 205 GOALS — 26%
SLAP SHOT 179 GOALS — 22.4%

MOST EFFECTIVE SHOT IN THIS AREA:
WRIST SHOT 710 GOALS — 55%
SNAP SHOT 300 GOALS — 23.3%
SLAP SHOT 131 GOALS — 10.2%

MOST EFFECTIVE SHOT IN THIS AREA:
WRIST SHOT 721 GOALS — 47.9%
BACKHAND 262 GOALS — 17.4%
TIP-IN 254 GOALS — 16.9%

MOST EFFECTIVE SHOT IN THIS AREA:
WRIST SHOT 1,270 GOALS — 53%
BACKHAND 345 GOALS — 14.4%
TIP-IN 322 GOALS — 13.4%

49% all goals scored in the NHL last year came from Wrist Shots
5% other
9% tip-in
14% snapshot
12% slapshot
10% deflection
1% wrap-around

Source: NHL

Goalies have a hard time anticipating the trajectory of a backhand shot.

The backhand's advantage is its unpredictability. Coming off the convex blade can send the puck in any direction. Ideally, shooters start with the puck on the heel of the blade where it attaches to the shaft. They then move the bottom hand forcefully backward in the direction of the net while transferring weight from the back skate to the front skate. As they complete the motion, shooters should turn the blade toward the net so it ends up perpendicular to the ice. Depending on how long the puck maintains contact on the convex blade, it may or may not spin. Sometimes it ends up rotating end-over-end instead of spinning around its center. Goalies cannot predict accurately what a backhand shot will do, which makes it tough to stop.

Text-Dependent Questions:

1. Name three materials used to make composite sticks.

2. What is the formula for angular momentum

3. What percentage of goals inside 20 ft. (6 m) is scored on the backhand?

Research Project:

Are the best goal scorers also the best shooters? Do some research and determine which NHL players have scored the most goals in the past five seasons. Record their goal totals and their shooting percentages. Then research which players have the best shooting percentages in the past five seasons. Are any of these players the same? Draw a conclusion about who the best shooters are when accounting for both shot volume and shot success rate.

WORDS TO UNDERSTAND

flat-footed: not ready; unprepared

parallelogram: a quadrilateral with opposite sides extending in the same direction and equal

ricochet: to bounce or skip with or as if with a glancing rebound

CHAPTER 3

PASSING

Shooters frequently create their own shots, meaning that they will carry the puck into the attacking zone and take a shot on net without help from a teammate. More often than not, however, a good shot is the product of a good pass or series of passes. The best players understand where on the ice is the optimal position to receive a pass and which pass is the smartest one to make. A big part of this understanding is knowing about angles.

Off the Boards

One of the most common passes in hockey does not involve the puck traveling directly from one stick to another. There are many times throughout a game where the player with the puck has a defender between him or herself and a teammate. In this situation, players often employ the strategy of banking the puck off the boards to get it around the defender. The bank pass uses the angles of incidence and reflection. The angle of incidence is the angle at which the puck hits the boards, and

Passing the puck quickly is a tactic that can make it difficult for the defense and goalie to adjust to the puck's position.

the angle of reflection is the angle at which it bounces off the boards. These angles tend to be equal, so players must take this into account when they make a bank pass.

Touch Pass

Hockey moves fast, so players need to move, think, and react quickly. There are many situations where players do not have the time or the space to stop and control the puck before a defender is on them. Other times moving the puck quickly is advantageous because it makes it harder for the defense or goalie to adjust to the puck's position.

In these situations, players can employ the touch pass, which involves angling the stick blade to deflect an incoming puck to an open teammate. To execute this play, players must quickly assess the angle at which the puck is coming toward them relative to the position of the teammate to which they wish to pass the puck. Players must then open their stick blade to the angle necessary to deflect the puck in the direction they need it to go. The passer lets the puck hit his or her angled blade, from which it will **ricochet** to a teammate in better position. This is just one example of how players are constantly thinking about and using geometry as they skate around the rink.

Vectors

Good players are able to visualize developing plays, anticipating where their teammates and opponents will be. Good passers know how to use STEM concepts to take advantage of anticipating correctly. For example, when it is passed, the puck has a velocity vector. It has both speed (velocity) and direction (vector). A long vector means a puck is traveling quickly. The longer the vector, the faster the puck is moving. On the ice, there are multiple vectors to factor in, because all the players are moving and have vectors as well. Players must account for all of these vectors. They must be aware not only of their current speed and position on the ice but also that of the other players and their vectors. That way they can calculate the eventual position of a teammate or defender so they can pass the puck to the correct spot. The perfect pass hits a player in stride, so passers must understand vectors to direct the pass to where their teammates will be rather than where they just were.

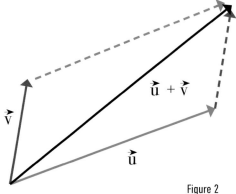

Figure 2 illustrates how vectors work in an on-ice situation. Imagine a player is skating up the ice with the puck. On the diagram, this player is located at the intersection of solid lines v and u. The player is traveling in the direction represented by the solid red line v. He wants to pass to a teammate on his right who is skating faster (has a longer vector). The pass must be made in the direction shown by the solid blue line u. However, the player must still account for the movement represented by v. Therefore to calculate the correct vector for the pass, the head-to-tail method can be used. Either putting the tail of vector u to the head of vector v (dotted blue line) or the tail of vector v to the head of vector u (dotted red line) produces the resultant vector u+v, which is the distance of the correct vector to complete the pass successfully.

What's Your Vector?

Hockey players use vectors without even thinking about them. For other jobs, vectors are thought about all the time. In the profession of air traffic control, controllers use vectoring to manage the flow of air traffic and to resolve spatial conflicts. They communicate vectors in the form of specific headings that divert aircraft from previously assigned routes. Reasons for this include adjusting the arrival sequence of incoming flights, avoiding hazardous weather, and simply helping with traffic flow. When vectoring is complete, controllers must instruct pilots to "resume own navigation."

Another way to make the same calculation is called the **parallelogram** method. Referring again to figure 2, vectors *u* and *v* are again the starting points. In this method, the dotted lines of equal length and parallel to *u* and *v* are added to form a parallelogram. The diagonal between the starting and end points will always be equal to *u* + *v*.

Of course, players are not mentally making these calculations in their heads as they play. Velocity vectors are something they have come to know intuitively from years of playing hockey, and they instinctively make the calculations in split seconds while moving at high speeds.

Saucer Pass

Another thing players—especially defensemen and penalty killers—do instinctively is to keep their sticks in the passing lanes. This means that these players are trying to disrupt opposition passes by putting barriers between the passer and his or her teammate. Another common tactic is for the defender to lay on the ice in the passing lane, making a pass along the surface impossible. To overcome these passing lane obstacles, players use what is known as a saucer pass. This is a pass in which the puck leaves the blade

When looking to make a pass, players must be aware of the vectors of all the other players on the ice.

John Tavares of the New York Islanders attempts a saucer pass in a 2009 game against Boston.

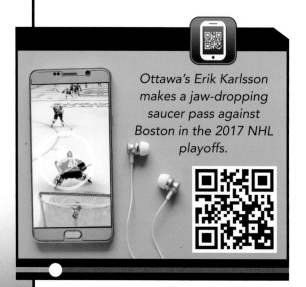

Ottawa's Erik Karlsson makes a jaw-dropping saucer pass against Boston in the 2017 NHL playoffs.

of the passer, travels through the air, and lands on the blade of the receiver. A University of Moncton physics professor identified four distinct elements to the saucer pass in 2017: spin (angular momentum), velocity, angle, and direction. The spin, as we know from previous chapters, is important because it allows the puck to be stable in the air, reducing the drag to make its trajectory more accurate. This plays into the direction element. The pass must be accurate, sent in the correct direction so that it lands where the stick of the passer's teammate will be. Velocity is key because the pass cannot be too fast or too slow. It has to be just right for the play to work. The angle may be the toughest element of the saucer pass. If the angle of the pass relative to the ice surface is too low, the puck will not get over the obstacle, be it stick or player, and the play will be broken up. If the angle is too high, the pass will get over, but it will take precious tenths of seconds longer, which may mean the passer's teammate is caught by a defender or gets in too close to the goaltender to make a play.

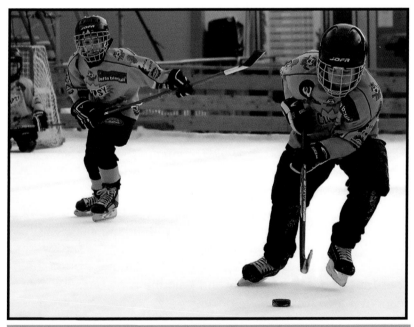

A young player prepares to drop the puck to a trailing teammate.

Drop Pass

The drop pass is most often used in the game when one of the teams is on a power play. This means that the opposing team has received a penalty and therefore is forced to play shorthanded for a given period of time. In these situations, the penalized team trying to kill off the penalty will tend to be less aggressive in the neutral zone, preferring to defend from its blue line in. The drop pass is effective in helping the attacking team gain entry into the opposition's defensive zone and set up its power play formation.

A drop pass occurs when the puck carrier is moving forward, usually with significant velocity, and while continuing to skate forward at the same velocity, leaves the puck behind them or nudges it backward slightly. Why is it effective to just skate away from it when you have possession of the puck? It would stand to reason that the defenders would just take possession of the puck for themselves. The answer is momentum. When a puck carrier is approaching the offensive zone with speed, defenders are typically skating backward, away from the puck carrier. When the puck carrier executes the drop pass, he or she either stops the puck's forward momentum or reverses it slightly. The defenders, however, continue to skate backward until they realize the puck has been dropped. They must then stop their own backward momentum before they can advance on the abandoned puck. By this time, the receiver of the drop pass, who was trailing the puck carrier with increasing velocity, will have reached or will be closing on the puck very quickly. The pass receiver is usually able to move around the **flat-footed** defenders easily and gain the zone because they cannot match his or her velocity.

To execute a drop pass, two players advance in what is known as an "I-up" formation, about three or four strides apart with stick blades aligned and parallel to each other. The leading player carries the puck and drops it by stopping its forward momentum with the convex side of the stick blade without slowing down. It is essential to ensure that the puck has completely stopped or perhaps is even going back toward the receiver slightly.

One thing to remember when making a drop pass or any kind of pass is that passers should never get caught looking down at the puck while making the play. At higher levels of hockey, any player with the puck (except the goalkeeper) is eligible to be body checked and therefore should be aware and on the lookout for defenders trying to separate them from the puck and their senses.

Text-Dependent Questions:

1. What does a velocity vector indicate?

2. What are the four distinct elements of a saucer pass?

3. What is a drop pass?

Research Project:

Do some research on a type of hockey pass called the "stretch pass." Explain in a short paper what this is, and detail its advantages and drawbacks.

WORDS TO UNDERSTAND

acrylic: any of a group of thermoplastic resins formed by polymerizing the esters of amides of acrylic or methacrylic acid; used chiefly where transparency is desired, as in the methacrylate resins Lucite and Plexiglas

conservation: prevention of loss; preservation

tactic: a plan, procedure, or expedient for promoting a desired end or result

CHAPTER 4

BODY CHECKING

In ice hockey, body checking is a legal defensive **tactic**. A body check occurs when a defender deliberately collides with the puck carrier with the primary goal of separating the player from the puck. Body checks occur constantly throughout a game, especially along the boards. Most are relatively unremarkable. The element that elevates a body check from unremarkable to the highlight reel is force.

Follow the Law(s)

Newton's First Law states that an object in motion in a given direction will tend to stay in motion in that direction unless acted on by an external force. Obviously, the puck carrier is the object in motion in our example, and the defender is the external force. When executing a body check, the defender is attempting to stop the motion of the puck carrier, or to at least change the puck carrier's direction to one that is different from the direction of the puck. The likelihood of success for a body check depends a lot on Newton's Second Law.

The main purpose of a body check is to separate the puck carrier from the puck.

Newton's Second Law states that the forces (F) on an object are equal to the mass (m) of that object multiplied by its acceleration (a), or $F=ma$. Acceleration is the change in velocity, and mass is the measure of the amount of material in an object that causes it to have weight. This means that the bigger the defender is (m) and the more his speed is increasing (a), the more force (F) there will be behind the body check. When two players collide, simple math determines which gets the better outcome. Will the puck carrier be knocked down or stopped in his tracks, or will the defender get run over? It all depends on which player exerts the bigger force.

Newton's Third Law states that for every action there is an equal and opposite reaction. This means that if one player exerts a force on another player, that other player also exerts an equal force in the opposite direction on the first player, or $F_A = -F_B$ where A is one player and B is the other. When player A collides with player B, they both exert the identical force on one another, in opposite directions, over the duration of the collision. This means

Watch Newton's Second Law play out on the ice, as some highly accelerated mass gets thrown around.

that as player A loses momentum, player B gains precisely the same amount of momentum lost by player A. Newton's Third Law maintains that the net change in momentum in this kind of example is always zero, a principle known as **conservation** of momentum.

Conservation of Momentum

Body checks in hockey are considered to be elastic collisions, meaning that the players do not remain in contact following the collision. In football, for example, collisions are often inelastic, as the tackler tries to hold on to the ball carrier. In an elastic collision, the outcome is determined by momentum. Momentum (p) is equal to mass (m) multiplied by velocity (v), or $p=mv$. The three most likely outcomes are as follows:

1. The two players have equal momentum, and both players come to a stop at the point of impact. This means that they both decelerate at the same rate, even if they do not necessarily move in opposite directions.

2. The puck carrier has less momentum than the checker and is driven back with a momentum equal to the difference in momentum of the two players.

3. The puck carrier has greater momentum than the checker, and the checker is driven back with a momentum equal to the difference in momentum of the two players. This may still be an effective tactic, however, if it causes the puck carrier to lose control of the puck, which may be unaffected by the collision and continues to move in the same direction and velocity that the puck carrier was going even though the puck carrier's velocity has changed.

In all three instances, the total momentum is the same before and after the collision. Since the mass of the players remains

Even if the checker gets the worst of the collision, he has done his job if his team gains possession of the puck.

constant, it is the velocity that is transferred from one player to the other. In the second example, the velocity of the checker decreases on impact, but the velocity of the puck carrier increases by the same amount in the opposite direction. The same is true in the third example but in reverse. The total momentum does not change. Conservation of momentum is expressed mathematically as $m_av_{ai} + m_bv_{bi} = m_av_{af} + m_bv_{bf}$ where *a* and *b* represent the two players and *i* and *f* represent the initial and final velocities.

Big Hits, Big Problems

A thunderous body check can be one of the most exciting plays in hockey. For most of the league's existence, an NHL player caught looking for a puck in his feet would often get blasted by a defender taking full advantage of the player's vulnerability to do maximum damage. However, with the evidence surrounding the consequences of head trauma and a growing understanding of chronic traumatic encephalopathy (CTE, which is a brain condition linked to repeated head trauma), the NHL has changed the rules regarding body checking to make it safer for players. Today, players in certain areas of the ice are not eligible to be checked even if they have the puck, and no check can primarily make contact with the head.

Location, Location, Location

Where on the hockey rink a body check takes place matters in terms of the impact the check could have on the player being checked. There are generally two types of body checks in hockey. Checks either occur in the open ice or against the boards. The boards are the 42-inch-(106-cm) high fiberglass wall sections that surround the ice surface, topped by the clear **acrylic** substance commonly referred to as the glass. Open ice refers to the rest of the 200 ft. x 85 ft. (61 m x 26 m) ice surface away from the boards. When a player gets hit in open ice, the check typically is more severe in terms of the impact on the player than one up against the boards.

Assuming both types of hits involve a full-on impact (not one where the checker only "gets a piece" of the puck carrier), the open ice hit tends to have a more devastating impact on the puck carrier because the puck carrier absorbs the full impact of the check. All of the checker's excess momentum is transferred to the puck carrier.

When the puck carrier is against the boards, however, he often gets sandwiched between the boards and the checker. In this situation, the boards themselves absorb some of the momentum of the checker. Those board-rattling, glass-shaking checks that look and sound so impressive are

The boards that surround the ice surface are designed to give on impact to absorb some of the energy from body checks.

ones that usually have little to no effect on the puck carrier, who hockey fans know will typically get right back in the play without missing a beat.

The boards are in fact designed to absorb force from impact. That is why they give and shake like they do when players crash into them. If they were rigid or more fixed, this would significantly increase the chance of injury to players. When the boards and glass flex and give on impact, what is happening is the duration of the impact (time (t)) is being extended. Rather than immediately bouncing off a rigid surface, the puck carrier maintains contact with the flexible boards for a significantly longer amount of time. The formula for acceleration is $a = \Delta v / \Delta t$, or the change in velocity divided by the amount of time needed for the change to take place. Therefore as t increases, a decreases, and since $F=ma$, force decreases when acceleration decreases.

Text-Dependent Questions:

1. What does Newton's First Law state?

2. What is the formula for momentum?

3. Why are hockey boards flexible?

Research Project:

Use the formula for force ($F=ma$) to calculate some examples how much force could be generated in theoretical on-ice collisions. Research the roster of each NHL team, and find the player with the highest mass. Then look up the average speed of an NHL player. Which two players would generate the most force in a collision? Next, look up the speeds of some of the fastest players in the league, and then look up their weights. Would the difference in speed above the average for any of these players be enough to generate more force than that of a heavier but slower player? Chart your results.

WORDS TO UNDERSTAND

akin: having the same properties

induce: to lead or move by persuasion or influence, as to some action or state of mind

neuron: a specialized, impulse-conducting cell that is the functional unit of the nervous system

stereotype: a simplified and standardized conception or image invested with special meaning and held in common by members of a group

vice versa: in reverse order from the way something has been stated; the other way around

CHAPTER 5

GOALTENDING

It is often said about hockey goalies that they are unique. Weird. A different breed. Oddballs. This is the **stereotype** of those who volunteer to stand in the way of 100 mph (160 kph) slap shots and would willingly stop pucks with their faces if necessary. Other than a certain perspective about the game, a good goaltender also has to have flexibility, good reflexes, and speedy reaction time.

Reaction Time

Reaction time is the amount of time it takes to respond to a stimulus, which for hockey goaltenders is a frozen rubber disc flying at them more than thirty times each game. Reaction time is calculated by dividing the distance from the puck by its velocity.

A shot from the blue line is a common one for goalies to face. Coming from that far out (60 ft., or 18.3 m), the shot is typically a slap shot, which can be as fast as 100 mph or 146 feet per second (160 kph or 44.4 mps). That means $d/t = .41$ seconds, which is the time a goaltender has to react to the shot before it gets to the net. Oftentimes goaltending in hockey relies heavily on positioning. If the goalie is well-positioned, pucks will just hit him or her. Those shots headed for the corners of the goal, however, require speedy reactions to keep the puck out, like the less than half a second needed to save a point shot.

Good positioning can cover up deficiencies in reaction time, and **vice versa**. The best goalies, however, work hard to have an excellent combination of both. Half a second is, in many cases, a luxurious amount of reaction time. A wrist shot from twenty feet out leaves a goalie with about two-tenths of a second to react. This is where anticipation comes into play, because the goalie will try to judge where the shot will go based on physical cues from the shooter and other situational elements. Goalies work hard in practice on positional play and shot anticipation. In spite of this, there are always situations where the goalie faces a miniscule reaction time, and it is often his or her reflexes that bail him or her out.

Shots to the corners of the net require quick reactions and big stretches.

Reflexes

When something is referred to as being a reflex, this means it was done without conscious thought. It is a response to a stimulus that occurs automatically. In the case of goaltenders, this automatic response is reinforced by years of training. It is not the training of the body in this case, however, but rather the training of the nervous system.

Reflexes are the simplest circuits in the nervous system, but they are unique in how they occur in the body. Typically, when action is needed, sensory **neurons** send information to the brain, which relays it to the spinal cord to connect with a motor neuron. The motor neuron in turn sends a message to the muscles, which respond by contracting or releasing as required.

In the brain, the cerebral cortex controls behavior. Reflexes, however, are not triggered from the brain. They are not conscious actions. Many goalies will say that if you have to think about what is needed to make a save, it is already too late. What happens instead with reflexes is that sensory neurons send an impulse to the central nervous system through the afferent sensory pathway. Instead of going to the brain, however, the impulse is sent instead directly to the spinal cord by what is known as the reflex arc. The reflex arc is a neural pathway made up of a sensory neuron and a motor neuron. When the impulse arrives, the arc's motor neuron sends it to the muscles through the efferent motor pathway.

Like other more common examples such as blinking or coughing, no thought is needed to complete the action. Reflexes just need a trigger—a speck of dust floating near the eye or a tickle in the throat. For goalies, the trigger is the shot (or perception of a shot), and their reflexes kick in without them having to think about it. Reflex impulses make their journey in as little as one-tenth of a second, which is why the best goalies come up with the save even with very little reaction time.

Shooting Angles

Goalies can count on their reflexes when facing fast-moving shots, but they certainly can make it easier on themselves if they are in good position. For goaltenders, understanding good positional play depends largely on understanding

shooting angles. This is one of the most basic aspects of learning to play the position, and it is really just simple geometry.

The premise of goaltending is simple: goalies need to put themselves between the puck and the net. The less of the net a shooter can see, the lesser the chance he or she can hit it with a shot. As the attacking team moves the puck around the zone,

Being in good position to have most pucks hit them is what goalies strive to do.

the goalie is constantly managing angles as the opponents shift multiple times in relation to the net. Goalies want to be square to the puck (lining up their shoulders to be perpendicular to the projected path of the shot) as much as possible and **induce** the puck carrier to do one of the following:

⇨ Delay shooting the puck while trying to find a better angle, giving a defender the chance to check the puck carrier.

⇨ Give up the puck by attempting to pass it.

⇨ Shoot the puck at a time that is optimal for the goalie to save it.

Figure 3

The importance of angles and positioning for goalies is explained in this short video.

The puck carrier's position on the ice determines the angle he or she has on the net. In figure 3, for example, player C has the biggest (least acute) angle, whereas player A has the sharpest (most acute) angle. The goaltender should play each of these potential shooters differently. He or she wants to cut down the angle potential shooters might have, and this is done by adjusting his or her distance from the goal line or adjusting the depth.

A goalie is said to be playing deep in the net when he or she is standing on the goal line. Goalies will be in this position when the puck is behind the net, or in position A. With the puck in position B, however, if the goalie moves to the top of the blue painted area (known as the crease), the shooter will be able to see less of the net. The same is true for position C. In this position, the shooter can see the entire net with the goalie playing deep. With the puck in the slot (position C), goalies should move out toward shooters to cut down the angle, giving them less of the net to shoot at.

Of course, there are dangers with playing angles too aggressively. For example, if the puck is in position C and the goalie moves out to challenge the shooter by cutting down the angle, this opens up the option of a pass to position A that will catch the goalie out of position. This is where goalies rely on their defense to cover players in their own end of the rink. Goalies focus on potential shooters and count on their teammates to take away passing lanes.

Goalies that play further from the goal line also must move further to stay square to the puck as it moves around the zone. As the radius from the center of the goal line increases, so does the size of the arc they must travel. Goalies are trained to be square first and worry about depth second.

The farther a goalie plays from the goal line, the more distance he or she will have to cover to track the puck and stay square to potential shooters.

STEM Careers

Maintaining a perfect sheet of ice to play hockey on is a tough job. Many factors go into keeping ice conditions ideal. The people who figure out how to do it are mechanical engineers. These professionals work on rink designs, infrastructure innovations, and refrigeration systems. Brendan Lenko of Custom Ice, Inc., has been building ice rinks since 1999 and has created more than 400 ice surfaces in that time. Lenko builds rinks of all sizes but specializes in small, private rinks for which he developed refrigeration systems that could be uprooted in summers and reinstalled in winters. If being an ice guru sounds cool to you, mechanical engineering is something you could consider.

Learn to Read

Angles, positioning, reflexes, and reaction time are all important elements in hockey goaltending. Perhaps the element that most determines how well a goalie will do against a shot is the ability to read the shooter. This means being able to pick up certain visual cues from shooters as they approach the net. Goalies learn to quickly run through a checklist of areas to examine on the shooter. With practice, running through this checklist becomes **akin** to a reflex in that goalies do it automatically without thinking.

Among the things the goalie is observing as the shooter approaches are the side the player shoots from (left or right), the shooter's hand position, the shooter's body position, the angle of the shooter's shoulders and hips, the distance of the puck from the shooter's body and whether or not that changes when the shot is released, whether the stick blade is open or closed, where on the blade the puck is located, and whether the shot is released high or low.

Given that reaction times are very often less than half a second, some level of anticipation must come into play for goalies. The best goalies already have a very good idea of where they expect the puck to go before it actually leaves the stick. Goalies like the Dallas Stars's Ben Bishop key in on the release point, as he told NHL.com.

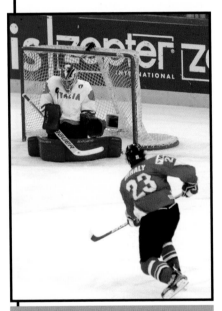

If the goalie can see the release point on a shot, he has a better chance of making the save.

"You'll see me sometimes stand on my feet making saves. It's one of those things you learn—you know guys in the League, their releases and where they like to go. If you can't see it (the release), you have to kind of go down first and react second, and then you are usually a little late."

Goalies like to see the release point. If they can see the puck coming off of the blade, that gives them a clue on the reaction they need to stop it. This is why teams try to screen goaltenders by standing in front of them to block their vision. It is not so much to prevent them from seeing the puck, although that is helpful to the attackers as well. It is primarily to prevent goalies from seeing the visual cues the shooter gives so they cannot properly anticipate where the shot might go. Today's NHL shooters are adept at changing shot angles and disguising their releases, so the ability of the goaltender to prime his or her reflexes by seeing the release and tracking the puck off the blade can make the difference between a big save or a dreaded goal.

Text-Dependent Questions:

1. How is reaction time calculated?

2. What does a reflex arc do?

3. What does "cutting down the angle" mean?

Research Project:

Test some of your own reflexes. Record the results of these three tests from Live-Healthy.com, then try them on friends and family members and compare results.

Sit on a table with your legs hanging freely over the edge to check your knee-jerk reflex. Gently tap your quadriceps tendon, which is located immediately below your kneecap, with a reflex hammer or a long straight tool like a yardstick. Look for a normal or brisk knee jerk that has one or two swings forward and backward, according to the New York University website. Repeat and compare responses in both legs.

Check your plantar or Babinski reflex by sitting on a table with your legs hanging over the edge and your socks removed. Rub the end of an object like a key, up and down your bare foot from heel to big toe. Look for a slight flexing of your toes. Note any abnormal response, such as your toes separating or extending.

Test your blink reflex by looking into a mirror. Bring your right palm toward your right eye quickly, stopping just short of making contact with your face. Repeat with the left palm and the left eye. Note if you did not blink.

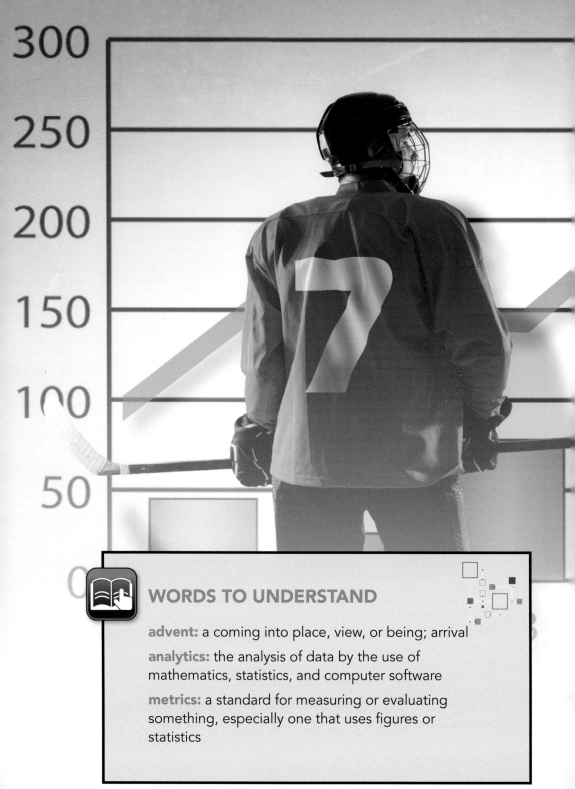

300

250

200

150

100

50

0

WORDS TO UNDERSTAND

advent: a coming into place, view, or being; arrival

analytics: the analysis of data by the use of mathematics, statistics, and computer software

metrics: a standard for measuring or evaluating something, especially one that uses figures or statistics

CHAPTER 6

STATISTICS

Like most sports, hockey is a game of statistics. From the traditional to the advanced, numbers are used to define success, determine which players are the best acquisitions for certain systems, and even to set the market value for players.

Traditional Stats

The traditional statistics for skaters (not the goalies) are goals, assists, penalty minutes, and plus/minus. Goals and assists are offensive stats, and plus/minus measures defensive success. Goals and assists are simple counting stats. Every goal scored is credited to a player, and the league tracks goal totals each season and over the course of a player's career. Assists are a counting stat as well; they are awarded for assisting to score a goal. In hockey, assists are generally awarded to the last two teammates of the goal scorer to touch the puck before the goal. If only one touched it since the last time the opponent touched it, or if the goal scorer created a turnover and was the only one on his or her team to touch it before scoring, then just one or no assist will be awarded. As with goals, assists are tracked and totaled by the league. In the NHL, almost all players end up having more goals than assists for the season as most goals come with multiple assists. Each goal and assist is called a point. To get a player's point total, simply add his or her total goals to total assists. Unlike goals and assists, penalty minutes count time. This stat is the total time a player accumulates in penalties. Penalties are assessed for breaking the rules of play and are given in increments of two, five, or ten minutes, from most to least common.

Plus/minus is a little bit trickier. For this stat, plus is a good thing, and minuses are bad. A plus player is a player who was on the ice for more goals scored by his or her team than goals scored by the opponent. All players on the ice receive a +1 when their team scores a goal, and a −1 when the opponent scores a goal. This is true only in even-strength situations. For example, when a team is penalized and forced to play with only four players, one team has a clear advantage over the

In hockey, penalty minutes are a traditional statistic that is tracked by the league. Fighting is considered a major penalty, which is assessed five penalty minutes.

other. In these situations, plus/minus does not apply if a goal is scored. It does not contribute to the plus stat of the goal-scoring team or to the minus stat of the team that allowed the goal. Teams must be at even strength, meaning that they have the same number of players (including goalies) on the ice for plus/minus to be counted.

Traditional Goalie Stats

Traditionally, goalie stats have four main categories: goals against average (GAA), save percentage (SV%), wins and losses (W/L), and shutouts (SO). Wins and losses are easy to understand. If a goalie starts a game and his or her team wins, the goalie is credited with a win. If the team loses, the goalie gets a loss. The combination of wins and losses is called the goalie's record. Shutouts are simple as well. If a goalie plays a game and does not allow a goal, he or she is credited with a shutout.

Goals against average is the stat that shows the average number of goals a goalie is surrendering for every sixty minutes of play. The formula for calculating GAA is goals x 60/total minutes played, and it is expressed by showing two decimal places. For example, a goalie who has given up seventy-five goals in 3,000 minutes played has a GAA of 75 x 60/3,000, or 1.50.

Save Percentage

Save percentage shows how many saves a goalie makes for every 100 shots faced. It is calculated by dividing the number of saves a goalie has made by the number of shots on goal a goalie has faced. For example, a goalie who has saved 2,612 shots when facing 2,900 has a SV% of 2,612/2,900 = .901.

Save percentage is considered by most experts to be the best measure of a goalie's performance.

This means that the goalie is saving just more than 90 percent of the shots he or she is facing. This statistic, the SV%, is usually regarded as the best indicator of goalie success. For example, a goalie who gives up just one goal per game will have a sparkling GAA of 1.00 and is likely to have an excellent W/L record, because most NHL teams score between three and four goals per game. A good W/L record and low GAA might not tell the full story, however. What if the goalie was facing only ten shots per game because his team is excellent defensively? That means his SV% is only .900, well below average for an NHL goalie. If his team were giving up thirty shots per game, which is more likely, the GAA would be 3.00, which is not very good by NHL standards.

Zone Starts

Not all advanced stats have to do with shots and saves. NHL statisticians track almost every possible aspect of the game now, including face-offs. We are not just talking about whether a player wins or loses a face-off either, although that important traditional stat is tracked as well. We are talking about zone starts. This is the number of times a player starts a shift in the offensive zone versus the defensive zone. Not surprisingly, players with high Corsi scores tend to also have higher offensive-to-defensive-zone start ratios. This stat has its limitations, however, because it accounts only for possessions that start from face-offs.

Advanced Stats

In and around 2008 saw the **advent** of **analytics** in hockey. The sport has lagged far behind trailblazer baseball and even basketball in compiling data and analyzing it systematically. Goals and assists were the hockey equivalents of hits and RBI in baseball. Yes, they told part of the story but only the surface. One-dimensional players could easily dominate goals and assists but might be responsible for letting more goals go in than they were creating. NHL team started hiring people who knew how to use math to go way beyond traditional stats to identify players with real skill who provided real value to the cause of winning hockey games.

One of the proven predictors of success at the NHL level is puck possession. Good players tend to have the puck more often, and teams that have the puck more often tend to be more successful. The godfather of devising **metrics** for measuring possession in hockey is Chicago-based financial

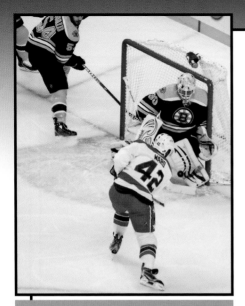

Corsi is determined by tracking how many shots, either on goal, at goal, or blocked, are taken by both teams when a player is on the ice.

analyst Tim Barnes. After hearing a radio interview with an NHL general manager discussing shot attempts and puck possession, Barnes, a part-time hockey blogger, invented Corsi, which he named for Buffalo Sabres goalie coach Jim Corsi because he liked a picture of Corsi with a mustache.

Corsi

The official name of the statistic referred to commonly as Corsi is shot attempts (SAT). It is designed to quantify shot attempt differential at even strength. This includes all types of shots: shots on goal (SOG), shots at goal (missed shots), and blocked shots. The stat is most often expressed as the Corsi For percentage (CF%). The CF% has two components, the Corsi For (CF) and Corsi Against (CA). CF measures the three types of shots taken by a player while on the ice, and the CA measures the three types of shots taken against the player's team while they are on the ice. To get the CF%, the formula is

$$CF\%=CF/(CF+CA)$$

A positive CF% is indicative of a player who spends more time in the offensive zone than the defensive zone, because shot attempts are obviously attempted on offense. A negative CF% indicates the opposite. A player who spends most of his or her time in the offensive zone must be on the team that has the puck more often than not while he or she is on the ice. CF% is generally between 40 and 60 percent, with 55 and higher considered elite.

Most hockey executives agree that Corsi is a more telling measure than traditional plus/minus of how a player impacted a game. Plus/minus is measured only when goals are scored, which is not that often in the grand scheme of a game. Shot attempts, however, happen all the time, and therefore, Corsi provides a much larger sample size for analysis.

Check out this Corsi crash course to get a handle on hockey's most talked about advanced stat.

Over the decade after Barnes developed Corsi, it proved to be predictive of success. The Corsi well is deep, because the stat is often parsed into situational subsets like Corsi Ahead, Corsi Even, Corsi Close, and Corsi Behind, which indicate games at different stages on the scoreboard. It is not all-encompassing, but Corsi study has shined a light on the underscrutinized value of possession and is now a highly utilized metric.

Fenwick

Corsi is SAT, and Fenwick is USAT, or unblocked shot attempts. Like Corsi, it is also calculated at even strength only. The formula is

*(SOG for + missed shots for) –
(SOG against + missed shots against)*

This is Corsi without the blocked shots. A hockey blogger named Matt Fenwick, a contributor to Barnes's blog, proposed that Corsi should not include blocked shots, because these were not true scoring chances. Corsi also penalizes a good shot-blocking defenseman, because every shot he blocks counts as a negative. The Fenwick For percentage (FF%) is calculated

Total Shots For/Total Shots For + Total Shots Against

The higher the FF%, the better. Fenwick scores have over time not statistically proven to be significantly different to Corsi, and teams generally tend to look at Corsi for individual players but Fenwick for the team as a whole.

PDO

The advanced stat commonly known as PDO is called shooting percentage + save percentage (SPSV%) by the NHL. PDO does not actually stand for anything. It is simply the online gaming handle of Brian King, who came up with the idea for the metric while contributing to Tim Barnes's blog. PDO is generally used as a team statistic, although it is calculated for individual players as well. King proposed adding a team's shooting

With a 3–1 lead in this game, statisticians for South Korea would be tracking Corsi Ahead, the team or player's Corsi when they have a lead of two or more goals.

percentage (SP—total goals divided by total SOG) to a team's SV%. His reasoning was that high shooting percentages and high save percentages were mostly the result of chance and are unsustainable over time. Therefore, players, but more so teams, with a high PDO are not as good as they appear to be and are bound to come back to the pack, just as teams with a low PDO must be better than apparent and will inevitably improve. A PDO significantly above 100 is considered high whereas significantly less than 100 is considered low. King argues that all teams will over time regress toward the 100 level. King expects teams with elite goaltending to be between 101 and 102, a number he feels represents the actual skill of the players.

Text-Dependent Questions:

1. What are the four most common traditional statistics for skaters?

2. What is the official name for the statistic commonly referred to as Corsi?

3. Which element of Corsi was excluded to create Fenwick?

Research Project:

Do some research into hockey's advanced stats and determine which players are the CF% leaders in the NHL. Then look up the players with the highest salaries in the league? Do the numbers correlate? Are CF% leaders that signed contracts in the last five years being rewarded with bigger salaries? Pick five players that make less than $8 million and explain why you would sign them to a big contract if you were an NHL General Manager.

WORDS TO UNDERSTAND

aramids: any of a group of lightweight but very strong heat-resistant synthetic aromatic polyamide materials that are fashioned into fibers, filaments, or sheets and used especially in textiles and plastics

errant: moving about aimlessly or irregularly

polymer: a chemical compound or mixture of compounds formed by a chemical reaction in which two or more molecules combine to form larger molecules that contain repeating structural units

CHAPTER 7

TECHNOLOGY

There is a lot of cool technology associated with the game of ice hockey, but literally the coolest may be the ice itself. How do you maintain a pristine sheet of ice year-round in any weather? Let's examine that and many of the other elements of advanced technology in the game of hockey.

Cold as Ice . . . but Not Too Cold

Modern-day ice rinks are a technological marvel, designed to create and maintain a high-quality ice surface in all kinds of varying conditions. The technology that goes into it starts well below the surface of the ice. The refrigeration system for a professional-quality ice rink has three main components: chillers, steel pipes, and brine water (a special solution that freezes at a much lower temperature than normal water). Up to 5 miles (8 km) of steel pipe are buried beneath the rink, where chillers cool the brine water to 16°F (−9°C). The surface of the rink is made of a concrete slab that contains several

To keep the ice nice and hard for hockey, NHL rinks maintain an ice temperature of about 16°F (-9°C).

pipes, which are filled with the very cold brine water to cool the slab to the desired temperature.

The slab sits between the skating surface and a layer of insulation that allows for the expansion and contraction of the slab as it adjusts to temperature changes when the venue might be used for other events. Below the insulation is a concrete base that can be heated to keep the ground from freezing so it does not expand and contract because that might cause the rink to crack. All the layers from top to bottom—skating surface, chilled concrete slab, insulation, and heated concrete base—sit on a foundation of sand and gravel with a groundwater drain. It's a complex, high-tech setup that allows for ice to be made and maintained at a temperature several degrees below freezing.

Hard ice is good for hockey, but it does not need to be twenty below (-29°C) to keep it cold. The ice that NHL games are played on is a fairly thin layer, which makes it easier to keep frozen. About 12,000 to 15,000 gallons (45,000 to 57,000 liters of water are needed to make a sheet of hockey ice, a process that looks like this:

⇨ The first two layers are sprayed onto the skating surface as a fine mist only 1/30 inch (.85 millimeters) thick each. These freeze almost instantly.

⇨ After the first two layers freeze, a third layer, 1/16 inch (1.6 mm) thick, is added. The hockey markings (blue and red lines, face-off circles, team logos) are painted on this layer.

⇨ The final layer requires about 10,000 gallons (37,854 L) and takes about fifteen to twenty hours to apply. It is added about 500 gallons (1900 L) at a time to ensure, smooth, good-quality ice.

The Zamboni

What do a WWII bomber, an oil derrick, and a Jeep have in common? All three contributed parts to the very first Zamboni. That name is of course synonymous with ice-resurfacing machines, which are commonly called Zambonis after Idaho inventor and entrepreneur, Frank Zamboni. These are the machines that put a shiny new layer on ice rinks in between periods of hockey games. He invented the first model in 1949, and now twenty-seven models later, there are more than 4,000 that exist in thirty-three countries around the world. The company has offices in California, Canada, and Sweden. Zambonis have handled the resurfacing jobs at Winter Olympic Games venues since 1960. Zamboni died in 1988 at age eighty-seven. He was inducted into the National Inventor's Hall of Fame in North Canton, Ohio, in 2007.

Modern hockey skates are a composite of materials to make them both lightweight and strong.

Equipment

Skates

Hockey skates have come a long way since the days when the Dutch strapped sharpened metal blades to their boots in the thirteenth century. Today's hockey skates are very high-tech. The boots are reinforced with a thermoplastic composite material, a polypropylene **polymer** that is woven into the fabric (typically nylon) of the boot to add strength and stiffness but is still lightweight. The blades are a mixture of titanium and pure stainless steel.

Helmets

The issue of concussions in collision sports like hockey and football has led to several high-tech advancements in helmets in recent years. Helmets have a two-piece construction, consisting of an outer shell and a liner. Both are made from a substance called vinyl nitrile, a foam derived from synthetic rubber. The outer shell is hardened and designed by engineers to disperse the energy of a collision across the entire helmet. The inner liner uses multiple layers of high-density vinyl nitrile foam that crushes on impact to reduce energy transfer to the head. Some of the

Here is a brief history of how Frank Zamboni's name became the one on every person's lips when talking about resurfacing a sheet of ice.

top-end helmets now come with a system where liquid-filled bladders are located throughout the helmet between the head and the liner that help to reduce rotational acceleration during impacts.

Pads

Hockey players wear pads over much of their bodies, primarily to protect against injury from being hit by the puck, as well as collisions with the ice, other players, and **errant** sticks. For skaters, these include shoulder pads, elbow pads, padded pants and gloves, shin guards, and jock straps. This equipment uses a variety of combinations of lightweight, high-density foam with hard plastic inserts.

Former NHL goaltender Jonas Enroth decked out in the latest goalie gear in a game for Dinamo Minsk of the Kontinental Hockey League, February 15, 2019.

Goalie Equipment

Goalies wear protective gear on every part of their bodies. A full cage covers their faces, and their helmets are engineered to withstand the impact of a fast-moving projectile. The helmet is made of fiberglass (sometimes combined with an **aramid**) or carbon fiber.

Goaltenders also wear a full set of pads, most noticeably a pair of large leg pads that cover the tops of the skates and extend up to the midthigh. These pads are 11 in. (28 cm) wide by rule and are made of synthetic leather stuffed with layers of both high- and low-density foam. The high-density foam is more comfortable for the goalie, whereas the low-density foam is for shock absorption.

Sticks

Modern hockey sticks are a high-tech composite of materials like carbon fiber, aramids, and titanium. Inflexible, heavy wooden sticks are a thing of the past. Carbon fiber is a very popular stick material, but it is not durable, so it is often combined with an aramid like Kevlar or titanium to strengthen the shaft and allow for superior flex.

Pucks

A standard hockey puck is made of vulcanized rubber, meaning the rubber has been hardened using a chemical process that cross-links its polymer chains. For the 2019–2020 season, the NHL introduced a decidedly nonstandard puck that can be tracked using microchip technology. Developed by a German company, the chips track pucks by collecting and transmitting data 2,000 times per second. The league will also track players with chips inserted in their shoulder pads. This will allow real-time information on things like the speed of a slap shot, how fast a skater is going, how much distance a skater covers in a game, and exactly where all shots are taken from.

With this innovation, technology has taken a big leap forward in the NHL. As league commissioner Gary Bettman said when the wearable tracking tech was unveiled, "Being on the forefront of innovation is good for our game, and most especially our fans."

STEM just keeps making hockey better.

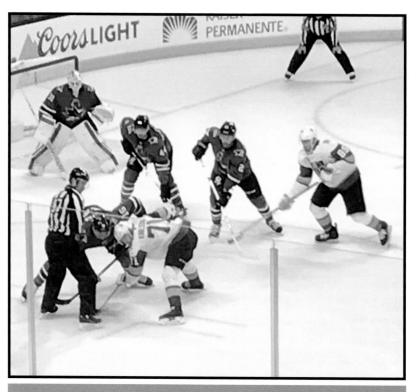

The NHL tested its new puck and player tracking technology in the regular season in a 2019 game between the San Jose Sharks and Vegas Golden Knights.

Text-Dependent Questions:

1. What solution is used to make the skating surface of an ice rink cold?

2. When did the Dutch invent modern skating?

3. What materials are modern hockey sticks made from?

Research Project:

A player's stick is one of the most important pieces of equipment he or she has. Do some research into the evolution of hockey stick technology. Note the time frame of major design and material changes and how these changes were implemented throughout the history of the sport at different levels. Present your findings in a two-page report.

Acceleration — the rate of change of velocity with respect to time.

Aerodynamics — the branch of mechanics that deals with the motion of air and other gases and with the effects of such motion on bodies in the medium.

Algorithm — a set of rules for solving a problem in a finite number of steps.

Amplitude — the absolute value of the maximum displacement from a zero value during one period of an oscillation.

Analytics — the analysis of data, typically large sets of business data, by the use of mathematics, statistics, and computer software.

Biometrics — methods for differentiating humans based on one or more intrinsic physical or behavioral traits such as fingerprints or facial geometry.

Center of Gravity — the point at which the entire weight of a body may be considered as concentrated so that if supported at this point the body would remain in equilibrium in any position.

Force — strength or energy exerted or brought to bear.

Geometry — the part of mathematics concerned with the size, shape, and relative position of figures, or the study of lines, angles, shapes, and their properties.

Inertia — the property of matter by which it retains its state of rest or its velocity along a straight line so long as it is not acted on by an external force.

Kinetic energy — energy associated with motion.

Mass — the quantity of matter as determined from its weight.

Parabola — a type of conic section curve, any point of which is equally distant from a fixed focus point and a fixed straight line.

Potential energy — the energy of a body or system as a result of its position in an electric, magnetic, or gravitational field.

Velocity — rapidity of motion or operation; swiftness; speed.

FURTHER READING

Haché, Alain. *Slap Shot Science: A Curious Fan's Guide to Hockey.* Baltimore: Johns Hopkins University Press, 2015.

Hynes, Jim and Gary Smith. *Saving Face: The Art and History of the Goalie Mask.* Montreal: Griffintown Media Inc., 2015.

Schottenbauer, M. *The Science of Ice Hockey: An Anthology of 28 Graphs for Kids, Teens, & Curious Adults.* USA: Createspace Independent Publisher, 2014.

Terry, Michael and Paul Goodman. *Hockey Anatomy.* Champaign, IL: Human Kinetics, 2019.

INTERNET RESOURCES

http://www.usahockeymagazine.com/article/2009-08/science-hockey
An article in the digital version of USA Hockey magazine, the voice of hockey in America.

https://www.nhl.com/
The official National Hockey League website including news, rosters, stats, schedules, teams, and videos.

https://thehockeynews.com/
Your inside scoop on NHL and hockey news.

https://www.hockey-reference.com/leaders/
An online resource for statistics on NHL hockey teams and players.

INDEX

INDEX

AUTHOR BIOGRAPHY

Andrew Luke is a former journalist, reporting on both sports and general news for many years at television stations in various locations across the US affiliated with NBC, CBS and Fox. Prior to his journalism career he worked with the Boston Red Sox Major League baseball team. An avid writer and sports enthusiast, he has authored over 30 books on sports topics. In his downtime Andrew enjoys spending time with his wife and two young children and attending hockey, football and baseball games.

EDUCATIONAL VIDEO LINKS

Pg. 10:http://x-qr.net/1Hvw
Pg. 23: http://x-qr.net/1Kqy
Pg. 34: http://x-qr.net/1Hx2
Pg. 41: http://x-qr.net/1JPR

Pg. 51: http://x-qr.net/1Kzx
Pg. 63: http://x-qr.net/1L0A
Pg. 71: http://x-qr.net/1Kdt

PICTURE CREDITS

CHAPTER 1:
© Philmarcelino | Dreamstime.com
Dustin_Byfuglien | Wikimedia Commons
© Romanotino | Dreamstime.com
photographer2222 | shutterstock.com
© Fifoprod | Dreamstime.com

CHAPTER 2:
© Katatonia82 | Dreamstime.com
© Rob Corbett | Dreamstime.com
® Justin Connaher
© Ondrej Hajek | Dreamstime.com
© Katatonia82 | Dreamstime.com
Mark Mauno | Flickr

CHAPTER 3:
© Katatonia82 | Dreamstime.com
© Alexandre Fagundes De Fagundes |
Dreamstime.com
© Jerry Coli | Dreamstime.com
© Jerry Coli | Dreamstime.com
© Milan P. Mihajlovic | Dreamstime.com

CHAPTER 4:
© Fahrner78 | Dreamstime.com
© Fahrner78 | Dreamstime.com

© Fahrner78 | Dreamstime.com
© Fahrner78 | Dreamstime.com
© Ivan23g | Dreamstime.com

CHAPTER 5:
© Bruno Rosa | Dreamstime.com
© Jerry Coli | Dreamstime.com
© Rob Corbett | Dreamstime.com
© Rob Corbett | Dreamstime.com
© Szirtesi | Dreamstime.com

CHAPTER 6:
© Sergey Khakimullin | Dreamstime.com
© Rob Corbett | Dreamstime.com
© Jerry Coli | Dreamstime.com
© Jerry Coli | Dreamstime.com
© Katatonia82 | Dreamstime.com

CHAPTER 7:
© Artzzz | Dreamstime.com
© Jerry Coli | Dreamstime.com
© Dmitrii Melnikov | Dreamstime.com
© Gints Ivuskans | Dreamstime.com
Daniel Hartwig | Wikimedia Commons